W9-BSL-933

Building our future together.

**MOSES LAKE PUBLIC LIBRARY
FOUNDATION** ■ www.mlplf.org

Working to develop, design and raise funds for
improvements to our public library facilities.

Like us on Facebook!

DO·NOT·DISTURB

DO·NOT·DISTURB

The Mysteries of Animal Hibernation and Sleep

BY MARGERY FACKLAM

ILLUSTRATIONS BY PAMELA JOHNSON

SIERRA CLUB BOOKS / LITTLE, BROWN AND COMPANY

San Francisco

Boston · New York · Toronto · London

The Sierra Club, founded in 1892 by John Muir, has devoted itself to the study and protection of the earth's scenic and ecological resources—mountains, wetlands, woodlands, wild shores and rivers, deserts and plains. The publishing program of the Sierra Club offers books to the public as a nonprofit educational service in the hope that they may enlarge the public's understanding of the Club's basic concerns. The Sierra Club has some sixty chapters in the United States and in Canada. For information about how you may participate in its programs to preserve wilderness and the quality of life, please address inquiries to Sierra Club, 730 Polk Street, San Francisco, CA 94109.

A LUCAS · EVANS BOOK

Text copyright © 1989 by Margery Facklam
Illustrations copyright © 1989 by Pamela Johnson

First Edition

Sierra Club Books/Little, Brown children's books
are published by Little, Brown and Company (Inc.) in association with Sierra Club Books.
Published simultaneously in Canada by Little, Brown & Company (Canada) Limited

Printed in the United States of America

Library of Congress Cataloging-in-Publication Data

Facklam, Margery.
    Do not disturb: the mysteries of animal hibernation and sleep/by Margery Facklam: illustrations by Pamela Johnson.—1st ed.
        p.   cm.
    "A Lucas/Evans book."
    Includes index.
    ISBN 0-316-27379-1
    1. Hibernation—Juvenile literature.   2. Sleep—Juvenile literature.   I. Johnson, Pamela.   II. Title.
QL755.F33 1989   88-10921
591.54'3—dc19   CIP
10 9 8 7 6   HAWK   AC

CONTENTS

1
BEEPERS ON BEARS
Scientists track grizzlies and black bears

A 300-pound grizzly bear shuffled through a dry autumn meadow in Yellowstone National Park. She stopped to catch a mouse with one swat of her huge paw and then ambled on toward a clear stream. At the water's edge she stood on her hind legs to look around and sniff the air before she plunged into the cold water. In a moment she caught a salmon with a swoop of her paw and gulped it down. She devoured two more fish before she waded out and shook the water from her thick, gray-tipped "grizzled" fur, which glistened in the sun.

Day after day the grizzly loped through the meadows in avid search of insects, berries, and small rodents, stopping once for a real picnic when she found the carcass of an elk. Food seemed to be the only thing on her mind.

But as she grew fatter and the air grew colder, she began to search for something else — her winter den. Like other grizzlies, who are the largest land carnivores (meat-eaters) in the world and are part of the bigger family of brown bears, she looks for a fresh new den each year. When she found a place that suited her, on a steep north-facing slope at the base of a large fir tree, she began to dig. Dirt flew as she scooped out a tunnel with her long claws. It was a tight fit as she tunneled under the tree roots that would make a strong roof for

her den, but she needed room enough only to squeeze through to her bedroom. In the spring, after four or five months of a deep sleep called hibernation, she would be much thinner.

The hollowed-out bedroom was just big enough for her to curl up in, head to tail. During her winter sleep, she would give birth to two tiny cubs, but they wouldn't take up much space. The cubs of a 300-pound grizzly bear are so small that they can both sit on a saucer.

For several weeks the grizzly crawled in and out of her den to arrange her bedding. Some bears use moss and grass, but this one liked the soft branches of a fir tree.

Late in November, when the temperature had dropped below freezing, the big grizzly no longer raced with the speed of a horse across the open meadow. Day after day she acted as though she were walking in her sleep. Her head drooped, and she dragged one foot after the other. Then one day, when

the wind whipped the snow in swirls around her, the bear crawled into her den. All night it snowed, covering the opening to her tunnel until it disappeared. No one would be able to find it. The grizzly was safe for the winter, cozy and warm beneath the blanket of snow. She would not eat, drink water, urinate, or defecate until spring. Her heart rate would slow down from its usual 40 or 50 beats a minute to 10 or 12. Her temperature would drop a few degrees, and she would breathe slowly, just as a person in a deep sleep would do.

Like their grizzly cousins, the black bears also sleep through winter, but they don't tunnel or dig deep dens. Some scratch out a hollow at the base of a tree. Others like to sleep under a pile of brush and fallen logs, and still others curl up in small caves. They, too, build cozy beds of moss, leaves, pine needles, or bark and branches that will keep them as warm as down sleeping bags.

Although it is easy to find the winter dens of the black bears, it is almost impossible to find the well-hidden holes of the grizzlies. For many years scientists tracked the grizzlies in hopes of following them to their hibernation dens, but it never worked. They lost track of the bears in dense underbrush or blinding snowstorms.

Grizzlies are nearsighted. They can't easily recognize a person more than a hundred yards away, but they do have a keen sense of smell. If they catch the scent of a human, the bears may charge. Dr. Frank Craighead, Jr., who studies grizzlies with his brother Dr. John Craighead, had several close calls. "Our lives depended on detecting the bears before they detected us," he said.

The Craighead brothers, working in Yellowstone National Park, learned how to trap the bears and put them to sleep with tranquilizing drugs. Then they had to work fast in the short time a bear was unconscious. With a strong nylon rope net, they lifted and weighed the sleeping

bear. One member of the team measured the bear while another took blood samples. They tattooed a number inside the bear's lip, checked its teeth, and attached a metal or plastic identification tag to the bear's ear. The Craighead team got to know the bears so well that they gave them names. There was Cutlip, Bigfoot, Scarface, Rip-nose, and Peg-leg, who limped on one stiff leg.

But no matter how carefully they watched these bears, they couldn't find their dens until they followed Marian. She was Number 40, and she became famous as the first grizzly to be tracked by radio.

In 1960 Marian was trapped and tranquilized. She weighed 300 pounds and was 65 inches long. The Craigheads put a bright red-and-yellow plastic collar around her 28-inch neck and attached a small battery-powered radio transmitter to the collar. The radio sent out beeps that the bear couldn't hear. But the Craigheads could hear the shrill beeping signal in the radio receivers they carried in their backpacks.

They followed Marian everywhere

and finally solved the mystery of where grizzly bears hibernate. Since then, scientists have followed many bears and studied many dens. They found that bears, like people, have different ideas of comfort. The tunnel to Marian's den was only two feet long. One grizzly den in Alaska had an S-shaped tunnel 19 feet long, with a bedroom shaped like an ice-cream cone six feet across and nine feet high.

In the years since radio collars like Marian's were first used, newer ones have been made that work so well that bears can be tracked night and day in the most remote places. The continual beeping signal can be picked up by receivers in a satellite orbiting in space, in a helicopter flying overhead, or in a truck on a nearby road. Many of the bears' dens are even "bugged" with equipment that lets scientists know when the bear moves or when the temperature in the den changes.

One kind of transmitter is no bigger than a quarter. It can be easily implanted under the bear's skin after the animal has been tranquilized. When the bear wakes up, it doesn't seem to notice that it has become a walking radio station that sends messages every time its temperature or heart rate changes.

The Indians of the Northwest honored the grizzly bear and called it The Bear Who Walks Like a Man, Elder Brother, and Old Man with Claws. One of their legends says it was the grizzly who taught human beings how to survive in the woods.

And now it may be the grizzly who teaches humans how to survive in space. If people could learn how to hibernate, it would make long journeys beyond our galaxy safer and easier. Hibernating astronauts wouldn't have to eat. They wouldn't need to use precious fuel to heat the ship, and they wouldn't get bored.

But there are many questions and many years of research ahead before we find the answers. How does hibernation work? How can animals go without food and water for many months without starving to death? Why aren't they weak and sick when they wake up in the spring? Why don't they freeze in their snow-covered dens? What signals them to eat enough to add layers of fat for the winter? What tells them it's time to enter the den? And then how do they know it's time to wake up?

Do hibernating animals have some kind of "magic potion" that makes them hibernate?

2
BROWN FAT AND THE
MAGIC POTION
How and why hibernation works

When Charles Blagden was a scientist at the Royal Society of London about two hundred years ago, he asked two friends to help him with an experiment. Dr. Blagden took the two men, a dog, and a raw steak into a comfortable 70-degree room, which was gradually heated to 260 degrees Fahrenheit.

Forty-five minutes later, when they

dragged themselves out of that hot room, neither the men nor the dog felt very good. All were thirsty and exhausted. The men were dripping with sweat and the dog was panting hard. The steak, however, was cooked.

It was a dangerous experiment, but it did show that living mammals adjust to temperature changes with some kind of built-in system. This inner system works like a thermostat, the gadget that senses when room temperature changes and switches a furnace or air conditioner on or off. The living thermostat is centered in a part of the brain called the hypothalamus (hi-po-thal-a-muss). Along with temperature, it also controls hunger, thirst, and blood pressure. And it is the hypothalamus that controls hibernation and sleep.

Hibernation is a way for animals to save energy and survive through the winter when food is hard to find. (*Hiberna* is a Latin word that means winter.) Estivation is a way for animals to survive the long, hot, dry spells of summer. (The Latin word *aestivare* means "to reside through the summer.") Some animals do both. The Columbian ground squirrel disappears into its underground burrow late in July and sometimes isn't seen again until March. It estivates and hibernates for two hundred days!

There are different levels of hibernation. The animals known as the "real" hibernators sleep so deeply that they are almost impossible to wake up. When they become dormant, their body temperature drops to near freezing. But even so, every few weeks the woodchucks, ground squirrels, and other "real" hibernators get up to nibble on food and use their underground toilet rooms.

Bears are the largest animals to hibernate. Unlike the "real" hibernators, they can be awakened easily. One scientist, who went into a den to see a dormant black bear, found out just how easily. The bear growled and started toward him. "I just punched that bear in

15

the nose," said the scientist. "And I got out fast." A hibernating bear can wake up fast because it has only to move around a bit to warm its body up a few degrees to normal.

The in-between hibernators really take only long winter naps. Skunks, raccoons, and a few others lower their body temperature a couple of degrees and breathe more slowly, but they wake up to forage for food between winter storms.

And then there are the "daily dormants," those tiny animals like hummingbirds and pygmy mice who can survive only if they turn down their thermostats into a kind of mini-hibernation every day.

In one experiment to find out how hibernation works, a biologist took a small amount of blood from hibernating ground squirrels. He froze the blood. In spring, he defrosted it and injected it into a different group of ground squirrels who had been running around full of energy. Not long after, the energetic ground squirrels curled up and began to hibernate.

Scientists have found in the blood of hibernating animals a substance they call HIT, which stands for Hibernation Inducement Trigger. Although they do not know exactly what this "magic potion" is, they have learned that this trigger goes into action when one of three things happens: when the days become shorter and there is less light; when there are big changes in temperature (either extreme cold or heat); or when food is scarce.

In order to survive weeks or months without food, most hibernating animals go on an eating binge in late summer and early fall. The fat they build up supplies energy and keeps them warm while they sleep. But along with this regular white fat, hibernating mammals have patches of special brown fat across their shoulders and back. The brown fat works like a fast-food restaurant. It delivers quick energy whenever it is needed.

A hibernating animal must warm up before it can wake up, and its brain has to warm up first in order to send messages to the rest of the body to get moving. In its handy location across the shoulders and back, the patches of brown fat are close to the hibernating animal's brain, heart, and lungs. These important organs, like the engine of a car, must get the first spurt of fuel, which is delivered by the blood vessels in the brown fat.

When a dormant ground squirrel wakes up, its head and front legs move first. Its hind legs are still "asleep" and numb because they may be fifteen degrees colder than the head and front legs warmed by the brown fat.

During hibernation warm-blooded animals turn down their thermostats until they become almost cold-blooded, and cold-blooded animals get so cold that they are barely alive. Hibernation is an amazing way for some animals to survive.

3
THE DEEP SLEEPERS
Woodchucks, ground squirrels, bats, and birds

Don't blame the groundhog if winter hangs on too long. Groundhog Day (February 2) is based on a legend made up by weather-watchers. Supposedly, if the sleepy-look-ing groundhog pokes its head out of its burrow, looks around, and sees its shadow, it scoots back into its hole and sleeps through six more weeks of winter. However, any groundhog who comes out of hibernation on a cold February day is most likely a male beginning to think of finding a mate.

Groundhogs are more commonly called woodchucks and, in some parts of the country, whistle pig or marmot. Like a furry bulldozer, the woodchuck loosens the soil with its sturdy front feet and kicks it backward with the long claws of its hind feet. It digs a straight shaft two or three feet down and then levels off to burrow a long main tunnel. It also builds several side rooms branching off that tunnel, including its bedroom and a small toilet room. A woodchuck seldom gets trapped in a burrow because it builds a front and a back door. A mound of dirt gives away the front door, but the back door is secret. It's the lookout hole, and it's hidden in high grass or underbrush, with no dirt pile to give it away.

Farmers and gardeners don't like the woodchuck, especially in August when the woodchuck's main job is eating ripening vegetables. It has to build a layer of fat at least three quarters of an inch thick, enough to last all winter and until plants appear in spring. Only in Pennsylvania is the woodchuck safe. There it is against the law to kill a woodchuck because it provides homes for so many other animals in its burrows.

As the weather gets colder in fall, the fat woodchuck heads for its bedroom. Before it got too sleepy, the woodchuck had built a soft mattress of shredded grass and leaves in the bedroom. As snow falls outside and winds blow, the woodchuck curls up in a ball and falls into such a deep sleep that it almost looks dead. Its heart slows from beating 80 times a minute to only four or five. Its normal body temperature of 100 degrees Fahrenheit drops to 45 or 50 degrees. You could roll a dormant woodchuck like a bowling ball across the field, and it would not wake up. But every few weeks the woodchuck wakes up and eats some stored food, uses its toilet room, and returns to its cozy bedroom to sleep deeply again.

Ground squirrels are also deep sleepers. In the cold, barren land of the far north, the Arctic ground squirrel spends only four or five months of each year awake. From the first freezing days in late September or early October, each fat ground squirrel is curled up alone in its nest of grass, hair, and leaves at the end of its burrow. Soon it is barely breathing and almost as cold as ice. Like its woodchuck cousin, the ground squirrel wakes up every three or four weeks, nibbles on its supply of seeds, and then goes back to sleep again.

By May, when the ground squirrel is ready for its spring break, the Arctic soil is still frozen and covered with snow. Until plants begin to sprout, the ground squirrel must live on its fat and on the leftovers of its stored food.

In its short life aboveground between spring and autumn, the ground squirrel mates, has its babies, and raises them. A newborn ground squirrel baby

is a grownup in thirty-nine days! Late in July, the ground squirrels begin scurrying around storing food and eating.

All summer, while the northern ground squirrels get ready to hibernate, the ground squirrels that live in the deserts of the Southwest estivate. They may spend the hottest, driest months of summer the same way their northern cousins spend winter, asleep.

The tiny chipmunk scurries in and out of its burrow in all seasons, unless it lives in the northeastern part of the United States and Canada. A northern chipmunk hibernates, but only after it's well prepared. Beginning with a small, narrow burrow when it's young, a chipmunk keeps working all its life digging tunnels and adding rooms. By the time it is four or five years old, a chipmunk may have 30 feet of tunnels, two or three rooms for storage, the deepest room for a toilet, and the largest room for sleeping.

In a bedroom big enough to hold a basketball, the chipmunk makes its bed of shredded grass and leaves. Even though its storerooms are packed with nuts and grain, the chipmunk tucks food under its bed until the mattress almost touches the ceiling. Whenever the chipmunk wakes up during the winter, it has only to reach under its bed for a snack. With an indoor toilet room, the chipmunk doesn't have to venture into the cold world until spring.

Bats are better than any electric insect zapper. In one night, a bat can eat its weight in insects as it swoops through the sky using the curve of its leathery wing like a baseball glove to scoop up food. Different bats have different ways of getting through the winter when there are no insects. Some fly south. Others sleep. Some do both. When the days turn cold, thousands and thousands of little brown bats fly to caves their ancestors have used for centuries. Others cluster behind the shutters of old houses, in

abandoned barns or attics, and in church bell towers. That's where the expression "bats in the belfry" came from.

By the time each bat is ready to hibernate, it has put on a layer of white fat and brown fat, doubling its weight from one quarter of an ounce to half an ounce. It clings to the roost upside down by wing hooks and toes, and wraps its wings around itself like a blanket before it sleeps.

Bats must winter in places that are neither too warm nor too cold. They can die if they get too cold, but they're also in danger if the air in their cave or attic gets too warm. If they warm up too often, they use their extra layer of fat too quickly and starve to death.

In hibernation, bats get so cold and stiff that it's difficult to tell if they are alive. But if hibernating bats are taken into a warm room, they can be ready to fly in just fifteen minutes.

Everyone knows that birds fly to warmer regions when they can't find food in winter, but who's ever heard of a hibernating bird? Scientists never believed the Hopi Indian stories about a

bird they called The Sleeping One until Dr. Edmund Jaeger and two of his students found a poorwill in 1946 in the Chuckwalla Mountains of the Colorado desert.

The gray and white poorwill, a cousin of the whippoorwill, was almost invisible against the gray and black granite rocks of the canyon wall, where it was sleeping in a hollow no bigger than a man's hand. Dr. Jaeger stroked the bird and even picked it up, but the poorwill did not move. Only when the bird opened one eye as he was putting it back did Dr. Jaeger know it was alive. Dr. Jaeger put a band on the bird's leg as a marker so he would recognize it again. He found that same poorwill hibernated in that same hollow in the rock year after year. The poorwill's temperature drops 60 degrees Fahrenheit in winter sleep. Its heartbeat becomes so slow that it can hardly be heard even with a stethoscope, and its chest barely moves with its shallow breath.

But when the spring sun warms the poorwill on the canyon wall, it bounces back to life like the other deep sleepers.

4
THE LIGHT SLEEPERS
Skunks, raccoons, and opossums

Many skunks, raccoons, and opossums have moved from the woods into towns and suburbs, where life is more comfortable. They like the leftovers so easy to find in garbage cans and gutters, and the wide choice of ready-made winter dens in barns, garages, and attics.

When winter comes and food is hard to find, skunks get sleepy. A winterfat skunk's usual brisk trot slows to a waddle, but it holds its fluffy white tail aloft like the plume on a bandmaster's hat. A country skunk has grown fat on a diet of insects, grubs, and mice, while the city skunk may have stuffed itself with bits of leftover Big Macs, candy bars, and dog food.

The country skunk's daily bedroom may be a hollow in the base of a tree or under a pile of brush and branches, but for a winter den it needs a deeper hole. Some skunks dig their own, but most skunks borrow a burrow. Usually without argument, they share space with other sleepers. As many as fifteen skunks, mostly mothers and their young, have been found huddled together in one den. Male skunks seem to prefer private rooms, and they often use an empty bedroom in a woodchuck's tunnel. Sealed off in its own bedroom, the hibernating woodchuck doesn't seem to know or care that its vacant rooms are used for the winter by skunks or other animals.

Even in a borrowed den, a skunk arranges its bedding of leaves and grass and plugs the doorway to keep out the cold.

A skunk sleeps more like a bear than a woodchuck. Its temperature drops only a few degrees, and its heart rate slows. It breathes in a slow, gentle snore, but it wakes up easily. Some female skunks stay in the winter den for a month or two; others don't poke their noses out until spring. The big males may sleep only three or four days, or simply ride out a blizzard and then get up to see what's happening outside.

City skunks find warm toolsheds or garages for their winter sleep. Disturbed by lights, noise, warmth, or the smell of food, city skunks seem to wake more often than country skunks. Or perhaps people only notice it more.

Skunks may be good garbage collectors, but raccoons are better. There's hardly a camper who hasn't had visits from the "masked bandit" searching for marshmallows and scraps. Raccoons scrounge around farms and knock over garbage cans in towns and suburbs.

The Algonquin Indians called the raccoon "arakun," which meant He Scratches with his Hands. Other tribes called the raccoon Little Man because its hands are so much like ours. But even with hands that can reach into nests for eggs, open latches to storerooms, or dig out the delicious meat from clams, the raccoon finds it difficult to forage for food in winter.

Biologists trapped some raccoons and put radio-transmitter collars on them as they had on the bears. They followed the beeping radio signals as the raccoons got ready for their winter sleep. As the days grew shorter in the fall, the raccoons ate and ate until they gained nine or ten pounds. While they added an inch-thick layer of fat, they also grew a thicker coat of fur.

Raccoons are restless sleepers. They get up often. The radio signals told bi-ologists that whenever the cold caused the raccoon's body temperature to drop lower than 96 degrees Fahrenheit, the animal stirred. As it moved, its heart beat a little faster, and it warmed itself up.

In northern regions, raccoons head for winter dens during the first snowfall. Snug and warm inside a leafy nest in a hollow tree, a mother raccoon and her cubs sleep together, while the male rac-coon finds his own bedroom or shares space with other males. The largest group of sleeping raccoons was found in an abandoned house in Minnesota, where twenty-three raccoons slept on ledges and between floor joists in the cellar. Another big group of raccoons denned under the pulpit of a small-town Methodist church. Raccoons love cozy at-tics, and sometimes the "ghost" noises people hear are just raccoons settling in for a long winter's nap.

Another restless sleeper is the North American opossum, which always looks as if it has just gotten out of bed. Its long,

scraggly hair is a mixture of black, white, gray, brown, and creamy yellow. While it is sleeping, the opossum folds its ears, making them look crinkled. No fur or hair covers its thin-skinned ears or its thick ratlike tail. If the opossum travels through snow or stays out in the cold too long, its ears and tail are quickly frost-bitten.

Like raccoons and skunks, opossums have moved into towns and cities where it's easy to find people's leftovers. An opossum can make a dinner of almost anything — insects, lizards, earthworms,

eggs, vegetables, or fruit. But with a wide variety to choose from, an opossum sometimes gets fussy. In one New Jersey town, an opossum helped himself to food at the birdfeeder, but turned down fresh raspberries offered by the home-owner.

An opossum can sleep comfortably in any kind of shelter, equally at home in a hole among tree roots or in a garage or attic. But it seems most at ease in a tree. An opossum is about the size of a cat, but it climbs better than a cat because it has five toes on each foot that grip almost like hands. Its tough tail works well as a "behind hand" especially when the opossum wants to reach out and grab a bird's egg or a juicy piece of fruit with its front feet.

An opossum never seems to be in much of a hurry, probably because it can get along almost anywhere. It has sur-vived longer than any other mammal. Its ancestors lived among the dinosaurs. If a human, a dog, or any other enemy comes near, the opossum faints dead away. Lots of people say it "plays pos-sum" or pretends to be dead. But it isn't really pretending. The opossum is un-conscious. Its tongue lolls out of its mouth; its eyes roll back in its head. It goes limp. A boy once carried one of these limp opossums around by the tail for a couple of hours, thinking it was dead. When he climbed a fence, the boy was surprised when the "dead" animal held onto a post. If the "playing possum" pose doesn't scare away its enemy, all the opossum has to do is open wide its big mouth, show its fifty needle-sharp teeth, and hiss.

Even though an opossum can act dead, it does not go into the deep, limp sleep of a true hibernator. Holed up in a wrapping of leaves, an opossum may sleep for several weeks of cold weather, getting up now and then to eat and look around. During the hottest times of year, this light sleeper may also take time out for a long nap.

5
THE COLD-BLOODED SLEEPERS

Red-sided garter snakes, lungfish, and frogs

On the first warm day in June in the Yukon, ten thousand red-sided garter snakes wiggle and stretch. At first they move slowly. They are stiff. For nine months they were buried under snow, coiled together like cold spaghetti, their blood as thick as mayonnaise. As the sun warms them, they begin to slither and slide over and under each other in their hurry to get out of the deep winter den.

Like all cold-blooded animals,

32

snakes cannot adjust their body temperature from within. When it's cold outside, snakes are cold inside. When it's warm, snakes are warm. And like all cold-blooded animals, snakes must find ways to keep from freezing or baking through the coldest and hottest weather.

The red-sided garter snakes live farther north than any other North American reptile. Their dens can be found from Labrador to the Yukon, above the Arctic Circle, where the temperature drops to forty degrees below zero Fahrenheit. In order to survive in the far north, red-sided garter snakes hibernate most of the year.

All summer long the snakes feed on mice, frogs, and worms. Late in August the females give birth to as many as thirty wiggly babies that look alike. They are born alive, instead of being hatched from eggs, and like all snakes, they know how to take care of themselves right away. Nobody teaches them what to eat or how to hunt for food. They know. They eat juicy earthworms until they are big enough to catch frogs.

Soon after the babies are born, the adult snakes start the journey back to their old winter dens. Shorter days and colder temperatures tell them it's time to get into the safety of a den below the frostline before the snow turns them into Popsicles. After only three months in the sunlight, the red-sided garter snake spends nine long months underground, coiled with thousands of other snakes waiting for spring.

Like all reptiles, turtles are cold-blooded, too. If they didn't hibernate during cold weather, they would die. Snapping turtles and other water turtles burrow a foot or two into the mud at the bottom of a pond or lake, below the frostline. The turtles won't starve because their dormant bodies don't need food, other than the fat they have stored during summer. It seems as though turtles would suffocate surrounded by mud, but they get enough oxygen from what has

been trapped in air pockets in the mud. Alligators also sleep away the cold spells in mudholes 10 to 16 feet deep.

Crocodiles and other reptiles that live in tropical climates must find protection from the searing midday sun or they would soon die. Many lizards and snakes burrow underground to estivate, which keeps them from drying out and overheating.

Most amphibians hibernate during winter or estivate during hot, dry spells. Toads and frogs burrow into the muddy banks and bottoms of ponds beneath the frostline, living on moisture absorbed through their skin. Early in spring, when the sun warms the mud, you can hear the chorus of toads as they crawl from their winter beds ready for another spring.

Everybody knows that fish have to live in water because they have no lungs for breathing air. Fish get their necessary oxygen from the water as it washes through their gills. But lungfish can live for months, even years, out of water. When they are in water, they breathe through gills like ordinary fish, or they can come to the surface and gulp air into their lungs.

In the parts of Africa and South America where the lungfish live, there are long dry spells with no rain. Lakes and riverbeds turn into hard, cracked mud flats. Ordinary fish would die, but lungfish burrow into the muddy clay. They curl up with their tails over their heads and secrete a gooey mucus that hardens into cocoons around their bodies. With all systems at their lowest levels, the estivating lungfish live on air that comes through a hole at the top of their cocoons.

Nobody knows how long a lungfish can stay dormant, but one lungfish was shipped from Africa to England in its muddy cocoon. After twenty years, someone put the brick-hard cocoon into water. The mud dissolved, and the lungfish was alive!

6
THE DAILY DORMANTS
Hummingbirds, little brown bats, and pocket mice

T iny warm-blooded animals live at high speed. The African pygmy shrew is so small that it can run through an earthworm's tunnel. Its heart beats 800 times a minute when it is excited, which is most of the time. To keep going at this top speed, the shrew needs a constant supply of food for energy. It works around the clock. Sleep comes in quick naps after a full meal of insects. Most of a shrew's life is spent underground, where it has no trouble finding food in the dark. Night or day does not matter to a shrew. Its short life is a never-ending round of eating and napping.

But the high-speed animals that cannot eat around the clock must find some other way to save energy. For part of each day, they turn down their thermostats and become dormant.

The smallest hummingbird is no bigger than a bumblebee, and when it's drinking nectar from a flower, it looks more like an insect than a bird. The humming sound is made by the whir of its wings beating so fast that they blurr as they move in a figure-eight pattern 60 times each second. A hummingbird can shoot out of sight at 60 miles and hour, fly backward, or hover in midair like a helicopter, but it cannot walk. Its feet are made only for perching, which means it can rest only on a branch or wire or in its nest.

Like an aircraft, a hummingbird uses enormous amounts of fuel fast. During the day it feeds constantly on nectar and insects, but it cannot find foot at night. And it cannot store extra fat for energy because a fat hummingbird would find it hard to hover in midair! So every night, when it returns to its nest, the hummingbird becomes dormant. It falls into a kind of mini-hibernation that allows it to rest without using so much energy. Its body becomes stiff, but in the warm morning sun, the hummingbird goes into high gear, ready for another day of eating.

Bats also live at high speed. They hibernate during the winter, but they are also daily dormants. The schedule of bats is the opposite of the schedule of hummingbirds. Because they catch insects at night, bats become dormant during the day. The little brown bats seem to like the attic of a house or barn for their daily roost. Early in the morning, the bats hang together in tight clusters among the raf-

ters at the peak of an attic. But as the sun warms the attic, the bats move down along the rafters away from one another and away from the peak. If they get too warm, they will come out of their dormant state too soon, and they will have to go back to work catching insects.

Not many animals are out and about on a hot summer day in the desert when the temperature can get to 125 degrees Fahrenheit in the shade. The little pocket mouse, which weighs no more than a dime, scurries around in the cool of dusk to find food. It shoves seeds into its fur-lined cheek pouches so fast that its paws seem only a blur. Just when it looks as though the pockets will burst, the mouse races down a tunnel to its storeroom, where it empties its cheeks and hurries back to find more food. The pocket mouse works and eats most of the night. At sunrise it scurries into its burrow and plugs the hole to keep out heat and snakes. Like the bat, the pocket mouse turns down its thermostat and becomes dormant for the day.

7
KITTEN DREAMS AND FISH PAJAMAS

What happens during sleep? Do animals dream?

S leep is almost as mysterious as hibernation. Sometime during the earth's twenty-four-hour cycle, as day turns to night, animals turn down their thermostats to save energy and rest. They are following their *cir-cadian* rhythm, which means "about a day." Like the deeper, longer sleep of hibernation, daily sleep is controlled by the part of the brain called the hypo-thalamus.

We don't just close our eyes and,

zap, we're asleep. Like all sleeping animals, we humans follow a built-in pattern. In the first five or six minutes, as we drift off to sleep, we still hear sounds around us. During the next deeper level of sleep, if someone wakes us up, we may think we haven't really been asleep yet. But in the third level, we are sound asleep. Our heart beats more slowly, our blood pressure drops, and our temperature goes down a degree or two. In the fourth level of sleep, it is even harder to wake up. This is the time when a growth chemical is at work (children really do grow overnight!) and damaged cells are repaired. It is also the time when we may walk or talk in our sleep or have nightmares.

We are dormant. We turn down our thermostats a bit, but we are never really unconscious. Like a bear in its winter den, we can wake up quickly. At a touch, the buzz of a mosquito, a stab of pain, or the smell of smoke, we are wide awake.

About every ninety minutes during the night we dream. Everyone dreams, even if one doesn't remember in the morning. Dream time is called REM (Rapid Eye Movement) sleep because our eyes move back and forth just as though we're watching a movie screen. During REM sleep, our hearts beat faster, we breathe faster, and our blood pressure goes up. Just before we begin to dream, we shift and move in bed as though we're trying to get comfortable before the dream "movie" begins.

Our first dream of the night lasts about ten minutes, but as the night wears on, one dream may last an hour or more. If we are awakened during a dream, we make up for it with longer dreams when we go back to sleep again. We have to dream. Dreams help us sort out all the information that has bombarded our brains during the day. Some of it will be stored, and we'll remember it forever; some of it will be forgotten.

Scientists were surprised when they

discovered that tiny babies dream half the time they are asleep. Newborn infants can't talk or understand what's said to them; what information would they have to sort out in a dream? Infants' dreams seem to be practice time, when their brains are poked and prodded by dreams to help them grow and develop. Perhaps baby dreams hold some kind of inherited, built-in instructions to help a baby learn how to use its new mind and body.

Imagine their even bigger surprise when scientists discovered that newborn kittens, rats, and rabbits spend almost all their sleeping time in this REM (dream)

stage. What do they dream about? Nobody knows, but it may be that, like infants', their brains are being prodded to grow and develop with inherited information, too.

Cats sleep away more than half their lives. You can sometimes tell when a cat is dreaming because it may hiss or arch its back. Dreaming dogs may twitch and bark or sniff as though they're enjoying a chase. Birds dream, too, and once in a while a caged bird can be heard to chirp or sing even though its eyes are tightly closed. (A bird can sleep perched on a branch or wire without falling off because its feet have tendons that lock the muscles automatically when the bird hunches down. When the bird wakes up, it has to stand up to unlock its feet before it can fly away.)

Amphibians, reptiles, and fish sleep, but they do not dream. An alligator basking in the hot sun dreams of nothing at all. It's hard to tell if a snake is sleeping because its eyes are always open. It has no eyelids. Sharks cannot blink or close their eyes either. When a shark sleeps, it has to keep moving in order to breathe. Oxygen-rich water must flow constantly into its mouth and out through its gills. A shark resting on the ocean bottom has to pump water over its gills, and that takes more energy than leisurely swimming.

The clown fish wears pajamas. At home among the brightly colored coral reefs in warm oceans, the orange and white-spotted clown fish spins a cocoon of slimy mucus around itself every night. Nobody knows why, but it may be that the gooey pajamas don't taste good, and bigger fish won't use the sleeping clown fish for a midnight snack.

Ocean mammals have to remember to breathe while they sleep. If they don't come up for air, they drown. Dolphins tend to sleep in groups called pods. A pod circles around and around, with one dolphin on duty, staying awake to remind the others to breathe now and then. Scientists think that a whale may sleep on one half of its body at a time. While the right side of its body sleeps, the left half of its body can stay awake to remind the whale to come up for air.

Sea otters sleep like boats tied to a dock. Each otter floats on its back with a long strand of seaweed wrapped around its body and clutched in its front paws to keep it from drifting out to sea.

Huge animals seem to need less sleep than tiny ones. Cows and sheep can manage with almost no sleep at all, but they do spend a lot of time resting while they chew their cuds. If we tried to sleep

standing up like horses do, we'd fall down. When a horse relaxes, the joints in its legs lock in place. Most horses are more comfortable standing as they sleep because when they lie down, their weight presses down on their lungs, making it harder for them to breathe.

Elephants get by with catnaps. Although they spend eighteen to twenty hours each day foraging for food, they sleep only three to four hours, and they wake up every twenty or thirty minutes to check for danger. Most elephants in the wild sleep on their feet, probably because it takes a lot of energy for a six-ton animal to scramble to its feet in a hurry.

Animals use most of their energy while they are awake. To save what they can, they turn down their thermostats on a regular schedule, becoming dormant for a few hours, weeks, or months.

A cat dreaming on a sunny window ledge, a dolphin circling at the surface of the sea, or you zipped into a sleeping bag for the night — each animal follows the built-in pattern of its species to rest and grow during the twenty-four-hour cycle of day and night.

A grizzly wintering in a cozy den, a groundhog asleep in its burrow, or a lungfish buried in its mud hole — each hibernating animal follows the built-in pattern of its species to survive the cycle of seasons.

INDEX